Witness From The Grave

Tell Your Future Generations of
Grandchildren About Jesus, Post-Mortem

Dr. Marshall Angotti

Contents

To Grace, my beautiful and loving wife.

Preface

THE HOLY SPIRIT INSPIRED me to write this book for two reasons: to encourage you to proclaim the gospel to your future generations of grandchildren, *From the Grave*, and show you how to do it. I am talking about you accomplishing this up to 150 years or more into the future after you are "absent from the body and present with the Lord."

I was struggling to reach the Christians in America to tell them about the Lord's ministry, WitnessForever.Org. My normal social media method has been successful in African countries, India, and other English-speaking nations, but not in the USA. I prayed for several months for the Lord's guidance in this matter and one morning at 2:30 a.m., He woke me with His answer to my prayers: "Write a book to reach the Americans about WitnessForever."

My immediate response was, "Nope, not going to happen. I am not writing a book."

I argued with the Lord for two months, saying I did not have the skills to do that. My education was in the sciences—biology, chemistry, and physics. Not English literature to become a writer.

But the Lord ignored me.

I finally said, "Enough. I will try." I struggled to write a few pages, and it was awful. But I was able to negotiate a deal with the Holy Spirit. If you do the heavy lifting, and I mean all of it, by giving me the words to say for this book, I will do the typing. And that is precisely what happened. For example, at one point, I was typing away on my keyboard, and I knew I was making mistakes, misspelling words, forgetting commas, and feeling my fingers hitting two keys simultaneously. But I kept typing for at least three pages.

When I did stop, I looked at the text, and there was not a single mistake. I took a deep breath and again realized that the Holy Spirit was in charge here. Throughout this whole process, I cried. What the Spirit of God has put down on these pages you are about to read is very compelling. It pierced my heart over and over again.

In this book, you will meet Julie, a young mother celebrating her thirtieth birthday in the year 2132. I want you to look at Julie, an unbeliever, as YOUR fourth-generation granddaughter. You are her ancestor grandparents responsible for reaching out to her more than one hundred years into the future for the sole purpose of witnessing to her about Jesus Christ.

If the Lord tarries, who knows how dark it will be spiritually on this earth? The Lord is providing you with this "Letter of Witness" to reach future generations of your grandchildren with the gospel.

Does that mean many of your descendants may be saved? Yes, because all things are possible with God. Does this mean it will happen? No, because only God knows the future. As believers, we are God's ambassadors or agents on this earth. He uses us to accomplish His will. You will be placing Scripture in their hands. And wherever there is Scripture, you will find the Holy Spirit convicting people of their sins and giving them the faith to believe in Christ.

In Isaiah 55:11 we read, "So is my word that goes out from my mouth: It will not return to me empty but will accomplish what I desire and achieve the purpose for which I sent it."

Can you imagine being in heaven and meeting several of your descendants' grandchildren, who are telling you with joy and excitement about their salvation? And that salvation was initiated by you, sending them this Letter of Witness from the Grave.

Let's join Julie on her special birthday, shall we?

Dr. Marshall Angotti
York, PA
April 17, 2024

Chapter 1

Julie's Thirtieth Birthday

IT ALL STARTED ON my thirtieth birthday . . .

Oh, no, I've overslept! It's 9:00. I'm in big trouble! Wait! No! Wait! It's Saturday! The weekend! My birthday weekend! And I don't have to go to work and teach those spoiled high school kids American history. They couldn't care less. Only interested in graduating this year and trying to get away from Mom and Dad. They are in for a rude awakening.

Have to go to the bathroom, bad. Now I can get cleaned up and go downstairs. It's awfully quiet down there. I wonder what that husband of mine, James, and our twin boys have cooked up for me? Actually, how big of a mess do I have to clean up?

I need to wash my face and wake up. I am afraid to look in the mirror and, for the first time, see what I, Julie Russo-White, looks like at age thirty. Ugh, how did this happen so fast? It seems that just yesterday, I turned twenty-one. And here I am, an old married woman with twin boys. This is depressing. Just get dressed and face the music.

1

"I hear her coming down the steps; get ready," said James to the boys. "Now! Happy birthday to you. Come on, boys, help me sing "Happy Birthday" to your mom. It's a big one, thirty years old today. She's a little sad about hitting thirty, so help me sing to make her smile. Okay, ready?"

"Happy birthday to you, happy birthday to you.

Happy birthday to Mommy and Julie, and happy birthday to you.

"Yay for Mommy. We love you, Mommy."

"See, sweetheart, it's not so bad. Being thirty years old in the year 2132, it's pretty cool. The twins are six years old. During the births, the first two years with no sleep, being completely exhausted. Preschool. Kindergarten. You survived all of that. Hey, the next thirty years will be cake. Really, what could be as difficult as all of that?

"Speaking of cake, look at what the boys bought for you, Julie. Your favorite. Red velvet cake. Three layers. Plus, your coffee-flavored ice cream. Plus, real whipped cream. Plus, dark chocolate."

"James, enough," I said, waving my hands in the air. "I am tickled pink, ecstatic, over the moon."

James continued excitedly, "Gee, we haven't even gotten to the gifts yet. Boys, entertain your mom, and I will find her birthday present. Here it is, hiding from me under the bed. For the most beautiful thirty-year-old woman, mom, and wife in the world. Super hot, indeed!"

"James, give me the gift, but keep telling me how gorgeous I am. I love it when you shower me with compliments. Please continue, sir, while I unwrap your gift. *Oh.* This gift wrapping is fabulous. You didn't do it but paid for it, right?"

James nodded in agreement.

"I thought so. You must love me, my dear husband."

James nodded in agreement.

"Open it, Mommy. Open it. Hurry!" yelled the twins.

Slowly, methodically unwrapping the box so as not to damage the paper and ribbon, I worked on my birthday gift. Finally, I removed the white tissue paper and saw this beautiful dress I had wanted for six months. It is the latest design and concept based on the new fabric, *shez*FAB: long sleeves, vertical collar, mid-thigh. After having the garment on for five minutes, the fabric senses the skin's temperature, and when it reaches 95 degrees, the average temp of the skin, the fabric gently shrinks to the shape of the person's body. A hidden zipper down the middle of the front of the dress allows for a more risqué option—plus lightweight knee-high boots made of the same material and color as the garment.

By the way, my color is, you guessed it, electric red. I, in this outfit, will drive James out of his mind, which is the main idea. Right? And now it is mine. My entire mood changed for the better.

"How did you know about this outfit? How?"

"Well, my dear sweetheart, I sometimes pay attention to what you say and do. You let it slip about finding a gorgeous outfit online. I knew you would be surprised. Perfect for when we go dancing. You are going to look fabulous. But of course, Julie, you always look fabulous when we dance. You light up the dance floor. This will be an extra special evening for you. You deserve it, sweetheart."

James continued, "I also have a more practical gift for you that will make your everyday life easier and more pleasant. May I present you the newest, most advanced version of communications, the X-Comm 4.0?"

"Oh, James, this is perfect. I am so tired of my old 1.2 model. So antiquated and slow. Give me a quick demonstration. I want to start using it right now."

"Sure. Look at the design. Smaller, sleeker, with new features. This part fits in your ear, of course. This clear, thin band goes around the back of your ear to hold everything in place and also contains a lot of technology, the antennae, GPS, battery, etc. And this tiny tube coming out of the bottom of the earbud is the projector and camera lens. Many features stay the same as the original 1.0 version. Your account with all your data is stored in the Kosmos, formerly known as the Cloud, back when dinosaurs roamed the earth.

"Of course, you still have your original account and ID number. Everything is voice-activated concerning the commands and functions you desire. For example, Call James, Text James, Email James, or Video call James.

"Or speak the question: Find the best pizza deals on Thursday nights. All that could be done on the old cell phones and computers can be accomplished with the X-Comm 4.0. Because of this phenomenal feature, the projector tube, a hologram, will appear in front of your eyes. This is your new screen. You decide its size and placement. Allows you to see text messages, read emails, view video calls, view anything as if reading or watching a computer screen or cell phone."

"Wow! What about security? How do I know it's me?"

"Good question. Before placing it in your ear, hold the bud up to your eye for a security scan of your iris and speak your name. Also, the GPS will place you in your pre-programmed locations of permission to use."

"I am impressed."

"The doorbell is ringing," the twins yelled.

"Who could that be? It's Saturday morning. James, are you expecting anyone?"

"Nope. But I'll get it. Yes, may I help you?" James asked, opening the door.

"I have a special delivery for Julie Russo-White. She must sign for it. Is she home?"

"Of course. Julie, I need you at the front door."

"What is it?"

"You have a special delivery, sweetheart, and you must sign for it."

Wow, this is different. It never happened to me before. In-person daily mail delivery stopped decades ago when my mom was a kid. There is no need for it in a digital world, except for special occasions like today, I guess.

"Where do I sign? Okay, done. Do I need to do anything else?"

"No, ma'am. This is for you." He handed me a large stiff envelope.

Then he was gone, leaving me perplexed with this envelope in my hands. The return address is a distant cousin I remember meeting only once five or six years ago. Why would he be sending me something, especially today, my birthday?

I carefully open the envelope. It is so rigid. It must be protecting something. Okay, there are two letters, or not. Two separate pieces of paper, one a trifold. Wait, there is something stuck at the bottom. It's hard to reach in this stiff envelope. I feel it with my fingertips. It's flat, thin, and round. I have it. It's a coin in some clear sealed plastic case. It's so shiny. Looks brand new. Can you imagine having to use coins and paper money to make purchases? It's such an inconvenience.

But this coin is fascinating. Has so much history in its design. On one side, it says Liberty in large letters. In God We Trust in smaller letters. An image of a lady with flowers in one arm, a radiant sun and the year 2011. Wow, this coin is old. Right? It is 121 years old.

The United States of America, 1 oz., is printed on the back. Fine Silver-One Dollar, an image of an eagle in the middle of the coin holding arrows in one claw and a tree branch in the other claw, and some fine print I can't read. This coin says it is one ounce, but it feels much heavier in my hand.

I had seen pictures of these American silver dollars but have yet to see a real one, let alone hold or own one. How much is it worth?

There also appeared to be a letter.

Jan. 4, 2023 - Is this some joke? I asked James if he could believe I received this letter written over a hundred years ago.

I read it out loud to James and the twins.

Dear Grandchild,

We are your ancestor grandparents, Doctors Marshall and Grace Angotti. We were dentists, practicing together for forty years in Hanover, Pennsylvania, starting in 1977.

We want to give you two gifts today, your thirtieth birthday: an uncirculated, collector American Eagle Silver Dollar, minted with 100 percent pure silver, and more importantly, the gift of eternal life, the gospel of Jesus Christ. Being our descendant, we love you very much and want to make sure you understand this "gift" of salvation, which is available to you. Enclosed is an essay in the form of a trifold I wrote. Grace and I have prayed for you and this moment in your life. Please read it carefully, meditate on the words from Scripture, and allow the Holy Spirit to guide you to all truth.

We leave you in the hands of the Lord.

Love with Prayers,

Your ancestor grandparents, Marshall and Grace Angotti

What is going on? This letter from 110 years ago was sent to me. A valuable coin. This is too weird. Plus, an essay written by my great, great, great, great grandfather for my benefit?

I could understand the coin and letter. But that writing about the gospel of Jesus Christ? I have no idea what that is about. I have never heard a word, a good one, about this Jesus Christ. The name is considered taboo and should not be discussed openly. Most believe it is too offensive and divisive.

Putting everything back in the envelope, I mumbled, "I'll read this other piece later tonight when the boys are asleep when I have more time and some privacy."

James wisely decided that the twins should have a play date at their friend's home for the afternoon. He will pick them up at 6 p.m. He thought I should have a little time off "mommy duties" for my special day. He thought correctly. I spent some of the time on myself and modeled my new outfit for James, which thrilled him. The day went by quickly, and before I knew it, the twins were home, had their baths, and were ready for bed.

Finally, everyone was asleep, and I could hear myself think—time to read that trifold from my ancestor grandfather.

Chapter 2

The Trifold

I BEGAN TO READ from the trifold.

"The Guy on the Middle Cross Said I Could Come."

The Gospel of Luke 23:35-43, tells of two criminals who will be executed next to Jesus: the first thief believes Jesus and goes to heaven and the second thief rejects Jesus and goes to hell.

But how did this happen and what does it have to do with you?

You may have heard the question asked, *If you die tonight would you go to heaven or hell?*

This passage describing the crucifixion answers this question. The first thief has died, the one that Jesus said, **"Today, you will be with me in paradise."**

In our imagination, it is a heavenly interview.

An angel converses with the **first thief,** asking,

"Why are you here?"

"I don't know."

"What do you mean, you don't know?"

"I don't. I just don't know why I'm here."

"Did you go to church on Sundays?"

"No. "

"Did you obey the Ten Commandments?"

"What are they?"

"Were you baptized?"

"No."

"Then why do you deserve to be in heaven?"

"The guy on the middle cross said I could come."

"But what happened to the second thief?"

"We never hear much about him."

A few verses that give us insight from this crucifixion passage in Luke 23:35-43: "The people stood watching, and the rulers even sneered at him (Jesus). They said, "He saved others; let him save Himself, if he is God's Messiah, the Chosen One."

Another verse says, "One of the criminals, the second thief, who hung there, hurled insults at Him (Jesus): 'Aren't you the Messiah? Save yourself and us!'"

With these words of mockery, insults, and unbelief, the second thief rejected Christ shortly before his own death, which sent his soul to hell. How do we know this is true?

The Gospel of John 3:36 tells us, "Whoever believes in the Son [Jesus] has eternal life, but whoever rejects the Son [Jesus] will not for God's wrath remains on them."

This is further explained in a verse in the book of Romans 6:23, "For the wages of sin is death, but the gift of God is eternal life in Christ Jesus our Lord."

What does this mean, "The wages of sin is death?"

This is referring to the second death - spiritual death. Hell. There are misconceptions of hell. Some believe that in hell, "At least I'll be with my friends." Others believe there Is no hell. Matthew 13:49-50 describes hell: **"This is how it will be at the end of the age. The angels will come and separate the wicked from the righteous and throw the wicked into the blazing furnace, where there will be weeping and gnashing of teeth."**

Also. in Mark 9:48, "The worms that eat them do not die, and the fire is not quenched."

This is a way of saying **Hell is an *everlasting damnation.*** There will be no hanging out with your friends. Everyone is alone and in darkness. Hell is a place of anguish, remorse, pain, and misery.

FOREVER.

In comparison, what did the first thief do? He admitted his own sin when he said in Luke 23, "We are punished justly, for we are getting what our deeds deserve. But this man (Jesus) has done nothing wrong."

Romans 3:23 says, **"For all have sinned and fall short of the glory of God."** Not some have sinned, or most have sinned, but *all* have sinned.

The first thief also said in this verse, **"Jesus, remember me when you come into your kingdom."** This is a statement of personal belief. This man is saying, "I believe you. I believe you are the Messiah, the Son of God. I believe you will be resurrected, if you are going to your Kingdom." As a result of this statement of belief, Jesus said he could come., **"Today you will be with Me in paradise."**

WHAT DOES THIS MEAN TO YOU?

This belief comes from faith, which comes from hearing the Word of God and from the work of the Holy Spirit convicting our hearts of our own sin and our need for the Savior. I know the Holy Spirit is stirring your heart right now.

Why do I say this? Because of Hebrews 4:12, **"For the word of God (the Bible) is alive and powerful. Sharper than any double-edged sword, it penetrates even to dividing soul and spirit, joints and marrow; it judges the thoughts and attitudes of the heart."**

Do not push the Holy Spirit away as He speaks to your heart today, as the second thief did, but embrace this faith the Holy Spirit is giving you to be saved by Christ, for Jesus said to the first thief, "Today, you will be with Me in Paradise."

Remember the statement: "The guy on the middle cross said I could come."

God saves us from hell, but He also saves us *to* heaven. The Bible describes heaven in this way: Revelation 21:4, **"He (God) will wipe every tear from their eyes, and there will be no more death or sorrow or crying or pain. All these things are gone forever."**

Revelation 21:18-19 ESV, **"The wall was built of jasper, while the city was pure gold, like clear glass. The foundations of the wall of the city were adorned with every kind of jewel. The first was jasper, the second sapphire, the third agate, the fourth emerald."**

Quite a difference from the description of hell. This scene at the crucifixion is an example of all humanity. Some will be saved and go to heaven, and *all* the others will be lost and go to hell. _Both groups for eternity._ I will raise the question again: What does all of this have to do with you right now?

God is inviting you to come. Just as He did with the first thief on the cross. But you may be thinking, *You don't know what I have done in my life. There is no way my past can be forgiven.* And you are correct. There

11

is *no* way to be forgiven in our own thinking and with our own efforts. But Scripture says, Christ died for all of us. He paid our debt at the cross. Our sins are forgiven and will never be counted against us.

Acts 2:21, **"And everyone who calls on the name of the Lord (Jesus) will be saved."**

First John 5:13, **"I write these things to you who believe in the name of the Son of God (Jesus) so that you may know that you have eternal life."**

JESUS IS INVITING YOU TO COME. Romans 10:9-10, **"If you declare with your mouth, 'Jesus is Lord,' and believe in your heart that God raised him from the dead, you will be saved. For it is with your heart that you believe and are justified (made righteous), and it is with your mouth that you profess your faith and are saved."**

And how do you respond to this gift of salvation? With a simple prayer. Please, right now, say this short prayer from your heart:

"Lord God, I confess to You that I am a sinner, and I cannot save myself. I believe You came to this earth and died on the cross for my sins. I believe You rose from the dead and are now seated at the right hand of God the Father. Jesus, please come into my heart and save me. Amen."

If you said this prayer from your heart and you truly meant it, because the Lord knows your heart, welcome to the kingdom of God. Your position in heaven as a child of the Most High is secure and sealed with your name written in the Book of Life. We read in John 10:28-29, **"I give** eternal life to them, and they will never perish; and no one will snatch them out of my hand. My Father, who has given them to Me, is greater than all; and no one is able to snatch them out of the Father's hand."

The Holy Spirit now indwells you, and "He will guide you to all truth," John 16:13.

May the Lord, who created all things, bless you.

(Courtesy of: WitnessForever.Org)

My head was spinning after reading the trifold. There are so many unfamiliar words: sin, heaven, hell, crucifixion, resurrection, believers, justified, and the list goes on. It makes my head hurt. But something caught my attention. I don't know what it is. It'll come to me. I was tired before I read that piece, but now I was exhausted.

Chapter 3

Discussion With James

I WAS SO CONFUSED about this letter that I tried to discuss it with James. "You know, James, I am struggling with this letter from my ancestor grandparents. It's all so confusing and difficult to understand anything about it. Seriously, what does the gospel of Jesus Christ even mean?"

"I can't help you, sweetheart. First of all, I have absolutely no time. We agreed that I keep my job and return to school part-time to earn my PhD. Second, I have no interest in these spiritual matters. Both of us, at one time not long ago, completely believed in science as I did and still do even after that letter came. And you did as well. Science and no mumbo jumbo. Julie, are you hearing me? Science, science.

"Come on, sweetheart, you are an educated woman. A four-year degree, plus a master's degree in teaching history. In those six years of college, did you ever hear one professor say anything to support this Jesus Christ thing? No. Absolutely not. Just the opposite. Because that nonsense is dangerous.

"Over the history of mankind, religion has caused nothing but division, death, and destruction. It is a threat to modern civilization as we know it. We don't know a single person who is involved with that mess. We were warned to stay away from those cultish people. All of us were required to take several college courses teaching us about the dangers of religion. I am sure you remember.

"In fact, you were one of the most vocal students demonstrating against this ridiculous cult, Christianity. You almost ended up in jail one day. Let me jog your memory. You noticed a small group of these devoted Christians protesting the abortion clinic near our university. You quickly called several of your like-minded girlfriends to come to help you counter their efforts and prove to them they need to go home and allow all women the right to abortion without any interference from anyone, especially the insane Christians. Who are they to use their hate speech and say, 'All lives are precious in the eyes of God who created them'? And then to encourage birth for adoption instead of abortion.

"You were so upset with these people demonstrating that you got in their faces, screaming at them with such force that you were spitting on them. Do you remember what infuriated you the most, Julie? These people did not try to defend themselves in any way. They just continued walking back and forth in front of the clinic, carrying their stupid homemade signs and praying in low voices. Yes, that's right, praying to their Jesus.

"Their behavior made you so violently angry that the police who had been called to the scene were almost forced to arrest you. Yes, Julie, arrest *you* and not those crazy cultish Christians.

"And now, here you are telling me you are confused by this letter. You don't understand what it means? Who cares what it means? I'm telling

15

you, stay away from this stuff. This is nothing but trouble for you, the twins, and me. Are you having a lapse in your memory? Do you have dementia?"

"No, I do not have dementia. And you are right about everything I did back in my college days. That day with those Christians and the abortion clinic was one of the worst days of my life. I still have a feeling of disgust and anger over that entire situation. But there is something inside of me that won't let me forget about this letter. I mean it's my past grandparents writing to me, over one hundred years ago. Who receives a letter like that? It has to mean something. I won't bother you again with it. I'll figure it out. I am sure there is a logical answer, and I will be able to move on from all of this weirdness very soon, and things will return to normal. No worries.

*But then some of those words popped up in my mind, **"and everyone who calls on the name of the Lord (Jesus) will be saved."** Where did that come from? See, that is what I mean—saved from what? Hell? Why do I keep thinking about that stuff? Hell sounds ominous, even if it is not true! I don't want anything to do with it. I just want to learn a little bit about this Jesus. But how? Is that asking too much?*

Chapter 4

Digging into the Past

LET'S SEE WHAT I can find on this Marshall Angotti, 2023, York, Pennsylvania. I know I needed to go to a special section on the internet for anything over one hundred years old....

Found it. Oh gee, a lot of stuff. Here is a website named SaintsPray.Org. I don't recognize anything here. Just information about praying for each other. Who needs that, right?

Wait, here is another website. This one is named WitnessForever.Org. This link in bold says "Letter of Witness." I received a letter, maybe this will help. I'll click on it. **The Guy on the Middle Cross Said I Could Come.** Bingo! It's the same letter I received. Okay, now we are getting somewhere.

"Testimony." What is that? I kept reading.

Testimony

"I am Dr. Marshall Angotti, a retired York County, Pennsylvania, dentist and a sinner saved by God's grace. In the spring of 2022, my best friend, Frank Lopez, was killed in a highway accident. Our connection goes back to our families immigrating in the early twentieth century from the same small village of San Giovanni, Italy. We were competitors in sports since we went to different high schools, but our families were members of the same Catholic church.

"We attended undergraduate school together and became classmates in dental school. If that was not enough, Frank and I became partners in developing new technology for diagnostics with X-rays and imaging for dentistry and medicine. At this point, I was working full-time in our dental practice and an extra forty to fifty hours a week with Frank. I did this for fifteen years; Frank and I were close.

"God had found each of us prior to our joint business venture, and we had an agreement that whoever died first, the other would present the gospel at his funeral. A memorial service for Frank was scheduled five months after his death in our hometown, and I asked if I could speak.

Permission was granted, and I delivered the eulogy, but not how I planned. Unforeseen complications arose, the Holy Spirit took control of the situation, and everything turned out perfectly, albeit in a very unusual manner.

"My wife and I have a few grandchildren to whom we are forbidden to speak the name of Jesus. We have been praying for them for the last several years. Three weeks after the memorial service, the Holy Spirit woke me one night and spoke to my heart, 'You now have a way to speak to your grandchildren about Me after you are dead. Change the eulogy into a 'Letter of Witness.' After more leading and guiding by the Holy Spirit, the Lord's ministry, WitnessForever.Org, was established.

Blessings, Dr. Marshall Angotti"

Julie was surprised and intrigued. *Let me think this through or try to. The trifold I received is called a "Letter of Witness." It appears that*

Marshall was delivering the eulogy for his best friend Frank Lopez's memorial service. It seems the eulogy was more of a... What is the word these religious people use? Speech, no. Sermon, yes, that's it. A sermon about the gospel of Jesus Christ, whatever that is. Soon after, that sermon morphed into the "Letter of Witness." So that Marshall and Grace, after they die, can present this gospel of Jesus Christ to their grandchildren. Because they were not allowed to mention Jesus Christ to these grandchildren. Then, also inspired by the Holy Spirit, again, this is Greek to me, they decided to continue reaching future generations of their grandchildren in the same fashion.

And this is how I received my letter on my thirtieth birthday. Sounds like science fiction. And what the heck is this gospel of Jesus Christ? It's obvious this is very important to them. Maybe if I reread the trifold, it will make more sense.

"The Guy On the Middle Cross Said I Could Come."

The Gospel of Luke 23:35-43, tells of two criminals. Who will be executed next to Jesus? The first thief believes Jesus and goes to heaven and the second thief rejects Jesus and goes to hell. But how did this happen and what does it have to do with you?

You may have heard the question asked, "If you die tonight, would you go to heaven or hell?"

This passage describing the crucifixion answers this question. The first thief is the one Jesus told, **"Today, you will be with me in paradise."**

In our imagination, a heavenly interview:

An angel conversing with the **first thief** when he arrives in heaven:

"Why are you here?"

"I don't know."

"What do you mean, you don't know?"

"I don't. I just don't know why I'm here."

"Did you go to church on Sundays?"

"No."

"Did you obey the Ten Commandments?"

"What are they?"

Silence.

"Were you baptized?"

"No."

"Then why do you deserve to be in heaven?"

"The guy on the middle cross said I could come."

"But what happened to the second thief?"

"We never hear much about him."

A few verses give us insight from this crucifixion passage in Luke 23:35-43 NIV:

The people stood watching, and the rulers even sneered at him. They said, **"He saved others; let him save himself if he is God's Messiah, the Chosen One."**

The soldiers also came up and mocked him. They offered him wine vinegar and said, "If you are the king of the Jews, save yourself."

There was a written notice above him, which read: this is the king of the jews.

One of the criminals who hung there hurled insults at him: **"Aren't you the Messiah? Save yourself and us!"**

But the other criminal rebuked him. "Don't you fear God," he said, "since you are under the same sentence? We are punished justly, for we are getting what our deeds deserve. But this man has done nothing wrong."

Then he said, **"Jesus, remember me when you come into your kingdom."**

Jesus answered him, **"Truly I tell you, today you will be with me in paradise."**

Another verse says, "One of the criminals, the second thief, who hung there, hurled insults at him (Jesus), **'Aren't you the Messiah? Save yourself and us!'"**

With these words of mockery, insults, and unbelief, the second thief rejects Christ shortly before His own death, which sends his soul to hell. How do we know this is true?

The Gospel of John 3:36, says, **"Whoever believes in the Son (Jesus) has eternal life, but whoever rejects the Son, Jesus) will not for God's wrath remains on them."**

This is further explained in a verse in the book of Romans 6:23, **"For the wages of sin is death, but the gift of God is eternal life in Christ Jesus our Lord."**

What does this mean, **"The wages of sin is death"? This refers to the second death - spiritual death. Hell.** There are misconceptions of hell. Some believe that in hell, "At least I'll be with my friends." Others believe there Is no hell.

Okay, that's enough. I should not have tried to read that tonight. The first two sections are more than I can handle. My head is starting to spin again.

Am I like the first thief or the second thief? Well, actually, neither. I am not a criminal. I never stole anything. Let alone did anything to be executed. This is ridiculous. And what does that have to do with heaven and hell? This brings up the question: Is there really a heaven and hell? Is any of this true? If so, why haven't I heard about this before? From my

21

mom, or in school? Why should I even care? Lots of questions here. It was never an issue before the letter came. But I am getting a sense of a warning. A warning nobody is talking about, so if people are not talking about this warning, all of us are being deceived. Who would want to deceive us, and why? On top of all of this mystery, I feel as if I am being drawn to want to know more. I can't put my finger on it. I'll figure it out. It shouldn't be that difficult. There is a logical reason for everything, right?

Chapter 5

Meeting Ann

"Hey, James, the twins and I are off to their soccer game. Sure you can't squeeze it in and come with us?"

"No, too busy with my PhD classes."

It was a beautiful morning for everyone to be outside. James was too busy with his PhD demands, so it was just the twins and me. I looked forward to these Saturday morning soccer games. It is so peaceful, with no stress, relaxing, sitting in my lawn chair and talking with the other mommies. You know, the usual stuff. Raising kids, dealing with finances, juggling a job with a family, and keeping my husband happy or trying to. Every family has their problems.

But this morning, I was chilling out. No worries. But I find my mind going back to the trifold. I made a few copies because I didn't want anything to happen to the original document. I am funny about things like that. I took it out of my bag and looked at the second page. That part about why the second thief went to hell has been on my mind lately. Please don't ask me why. It just is, and I can't shake it.

Here it is, **"Whoever believes in the Son has eternal life, but whoever rejects the Son will not, for God's wrath remains on**

them." So does this mean that you either believe in this Jesus and if you don't, you automatically reject Him? And what is this God's wrath thing? Is that the place where hell is being referred to? And who says hell exists? Anybody prove it? What happens if no one gives you a chance to believe? Then what?

The more I read this essay, the more questions I had. This mud puddle I found myself in kept getting more murky. I needed someone to help me understand this stuff. But where do you find these people who understand this information and are willing to explain it? I have heard and read about churches, and the conclusion was to never, and I mean never, step one foot inside those places. Danger zone. Brainwashing, big time. So that is definitely out of the question. But then this happened . . .

"Excuse me, hello, I am Ann, known as Grandma to that six-year-old red-headed girl on the opposing team. I noticed you have twin boys who are part of the next generation of great soccer players. Twins will keep you on your toes."

"Yes, and I do not have enough toes. Hi. And I am known as "the mom of the twins," but my real name is Julie."

"I am a twin myself," said Ann. "Looking back, I don't know how my mom survived. She already had two boys, ages four and six. Then she comes home from the hospital with two newborn girls. Can you imagine raising four kids under the age of six? What a nightmare. But she did it. I don't know how, but she did. And what a terrific mother she was."

"Wow. In my wildest dreams, I cannot envision having two older children to raise with these maniac twins. Your mom deserves a gold medal for surviving those years and achieving great success, from what you say."

Julie continued, "I attend these games regularly but don't recall seeing you. This your first time?"

"I come sometimes, not often enough. My husband passed away a few years ago, so I need to be around my grandchildren a little more."

"I am so sorry. Must be very difficult for you."

"It is, but I have great hope. My husband was a believer, so I know he is in heaven with Jesus. (My ears perked up hearing those words.) And my church family is extremely supportive and loving. I don't know what I would do without them, which brings me to the point of our conversation. I want to invite you to come to my church this Sunday. It is Faith Bible Church, on Straight Street. I've written down my contact information with the church location."

"Why would you come to me, a complete stranger, and invite me to do this, attend your church? Also, is it not discouraged to speak in public about such things? This could get you in trouble."

"That small, quiet voice in me said I should. And I have learned it is essential to trust and obey that voice."

Being caught off guard, I quickly replied, "Well, look, I am swamped, as you just said, and you fully understand with the twins and all. I'll think about it. No promises."

Ann nodded her head in agreement, we exchanged pleasantries, and she walked away.

What is wrong with me? I was thinking about how I was repeatedly taught how dangerous churches are, and I went right ahead and blurted out, "I'll think about it. No promises." I am such an idiot! But I couldn't help myself. It was like someone was speaking for me. Have I lost control of my mind and voice?

Ann said that small, quiet voice. That's a good way of describing what I have been going through since that letter arrived. What is happening to me?

After another few months of reading the trifold and having more questions, I contacted Ann and arranged a coffee. Not go to church but to talk with her; maybe she could shed some light on my questions. That's not violating my personal antireligion principles, right? I called it furthering my life's education.

Chapter 6

Ann Understands

"JULIE, TELL ME A little about yourself," said Ann.

"My younger brother and I grew up with a single mom. Our dad left us before I started school. My mom did not get around to telling us what happened, and she never remarried. I remember Mom being sad her whole life. So life was hard for all of us. Very little money. Only enough for the necessities. We lived in a small house. So, yes, not a great childhood. I did go to the local college. I always had a few jobs, borrowed money for tuition and books, and stayed home. I knew education was my way out of being poor. I studied hard whenever I wasn't working. I met my husband, James, when I was a senior. I never dated anyone seriously in my early years of college because I wanted to ensure I finished and got my degree in secondary education. I teach American History in high school."

"You sound like a very determined and disciplined young lady," Ann said. "You did not adopt the label of 'victim' but instead made the best of your situation. Shall I say, Julie, you rose above your challenges and focused on your goal? Bravo! You are an example of 'Where there is a will, there is a way.'

"Then you met your husband, James. Was it love at first sight?"

"It was for him. I needed answers about his family life. Did his father treat his mother with love and respect? Do all of the siblings get along well? How does he interact with children, nieces, and nephews? Is his family involved with any crazy cults? Will he have a promising career and be able to support a family with moderate comfort? After I was satisfied with all the answers to those questions, I asked James to marry me."

"You did what?!"

"Sure, I was more than satisfied with what I was getting, and I knew James just wanted me. Forever. I couldn't wait for him to fiddle around and try to pop the question."

I was starting to feel comfortable with Ann. She was like an aunt to me, someone I could talk to about anything. Kind, nonjudgmental, compassionate, and sincerely interested in me.

"Julie, I assume you have lots of friends. People who love you and respect you."

"I do. Not sure about the love and respect thing."

"Do you see them often?"

"Yes, well, often enough."

Then, for some reason, I started talking to Ann about this dark secret I was hiding in my heart. I don't know why, but I just did. Maybe it was the small, quiet voice. Who knows?

"I go out with my girlfriends about once a month. On one specific occasion, our evening out was to celebrate someone's birthday. We usually go to a bar, drink a few beers, dance with each other, laugh a lot, and go home.

"This time was a little different, a lot different. All of us drank quite a bit in college and continued after our marriages and having kids. We have maybe slowed down a little by not getting completely drunk regularly as we did in college. We had our beer and ordered mixed drinks for the birthday toast. I like vodka, so I ordered a martini. That's a pretty strong drink, but we usually have only one cocktail, wanting to be mature young mothers.

"We were having a good time laughing, telling stories about our kids and jobs, and dancing with each other, as usual. The waitress approached me with another martini, put it in front of me, and said, 'Courtesy of an admirer,' as she nodded to this fellow across the room. I looked, and all of us looked. Tall, dark, and handsome. That dangerous trifecta. I gave him a 'Thank you' smile. First mistake. This had never happened before to any of us girls.

"Every one of us knew this was a danger zone, but our judgment was clouded, being tipsy from the alcohol. Especially mine. I drank the martini and even danced once with the tall, dark, and handsome William. That was six months ago. We have talked on the X-Comm a few times and texted more. He is a great guy, owns several investment properties, and has a lot of money.

"I know it is wrong, but the temptation is strong. James and I are struggling with our marriage. He has been passed over a few times for a promotion at his job. His drinking has increased, along with his anger with the twins and me. So James decided to keep his job, return to school, and get his PhD in marketing. He would like to teach at the college level. This would get him out of the dog-eat-dog competitive world. Since this post-graduate work is part-time, we are looking at four years for him to receive his doctorate.

"On the one hand, I have this personal part of my life screaming at me, and on the other hand, I have this small, quiet voice gently telling me about Jesus." *And here I was, pouring out my heart to someone I barely knew as tears streamed down my face.*

"Oh, Julie, my dear Julie," Ann said as she held my hands. "Let me pray for you.

Heavenly Father, thank You for Julie. A beautiful young mother you created in Your image. Her heart is troubled by the challenges of life and sin. Yet her heart is also full of questions about You, Lord. I ask that You reveal yourself to her. Help Julie understand and embrace this truth when You say in Scripture, **'Come to me, all you who are weary and burdened, and I will give you rest. Take my yoke upon you and learn from me, for I am gentle and humble in heart, and you will find rest for your souls. For my yoke is easy and my burden is light'** (Matthew 11:28-30). And Lord, I pray against the evil that is attacking Julie. In your name, the name of Jesus Christ, I rebuke and cast out all demons who are tempting Julie to sin with alcohol and adultery. Leave her now. I command you! In the name of Jesus. Thank You, Lord, for Your love, mercy, and salvation. Amen."

In her soothing prayer, Ann used many words I had found in my letter and did not understand. At that moment, I felt more peace in my heart than ever before. *How do I keep it there?*

Chapter 7

Julie's Conversation With Her Mother

I FELT THE NEED to talk with my mom . . .

"Hi, Mom, this is Julie. Hey, can I see you? I need to talk to you about something. I know you are an hour away, but it's really important. Okay, see you this Thursday around 11 a.m."

It had been a while since I had been home. As I walked through the door, nothing had changed. The furniture has been the same for the last twenty years. It struck me how tiny our house is. I was always ashamed to invite any of my school friends over. We were poorer than I realized.

I see my high school and college graduation pictures on the coffee table. Of course, a photo of James and me from our wedding is on the wall. But something caught my attention that day: the picture of Mom and me on my wedding day. She had tried to smile, but her sadness showed through.

Entering the room, Mom said, "Julie, you have me worried since we talked. You said you have something important to discuss with me. Is everything okay with the twins? Are you and James having trouble with your marriage? What is it?"

"Mom, I recently had my thirtieth birthday and received an unusual gift. Look at this," I said as I took the envelope out of my bag.

Upon seeing the envelope, Mom immediately started crying. My mom never cries. This is the first time I have ever seen my mom cry. I put my arms around her and asked, "What is it, Mom? Why are you so upset?"

Between her sobs, she said, "Oh, I remember when I received that envelope. My life was upside down. You were four years old, and I had just become pregnant with your brother. Things were tight with money. But the biggest heartache was that I started to sense that your father was running around. And that letter arrived on my thirtieth birthday. I didn't know what to make of it. Your father yelled at me to sell the coin and throw everything away. He was offended by the letter. It made him furious.

"But something inside me said *No, keep it.* So for some reason, I listened, and I did keep it, and I have it, all of it, to this day. I didn't understand those things from the Bible, but I knew I needed to at some point, but not at that time.

"Chaos ensued. I am about to tell you something you don't know, but you need to hear it. Your father was unfaithful to me; as it turned out, my intuition was correct. He found another woman he was attracted to who had quite a bit of money." (Hearing this, I felt an arrow pierce my own heart, convicting me of my recent relationship with William.)

She continued, "To spare you the horrible details, he demanded a divorce, and we went through that awful process. I felt like a complete failure. My life was destroyed. Here I am, a single mom, a pregnant one at that, facing life with two small children. What man is going to want to marry me with two small children? So instead of embracing that gift of Jesus from our ancestor grandparents, I wallowed in my self-pity for years, decades, turning into a lonely old woman. And you showing me the envelope threw me back to those days of chaos and heartache.

"Over the years, I took out the envelope and reread everything, giving myself a sliver of hope. Tell me, Julie, do you think I have another chance to know this Jesus? Is there still time for me?"

My mind was going a thousand miles per hour. I had come home looking for answers, and here was my mom. She was stuck in this time warp of desperation and clinging to the hope promised in the words of the "Letter of Witness."

The victim of an adulterous husband and the unspeakable struggles of being a single mother, no wonder my mom is sad and has been heartbroken for most of her adult life. Not fair. No. Not fair at all. I must help her, but how?

And that small, quiet voice put these words in my mouth, "Of course, there is still time for you, Mom. We will do this together, mother and daughter, learning about this Jesus."

On my drive home, I thought about what my father had done. His behavior and decisions caused so much pain for so many people. And I was about to follow in his footsteps. But today, I had received a warning.

Later that evening, when everyone was asleep, I texted William for the last time. I told him it was over. I had made a terrible mistake responding to his advances. I told him not to reply to the message and not to contact me again. Of course, William immediately tried to contact me. So I blocked his number and ensured all possible communication methods were terminated. I felt a heavy burden lift off my shoulders.

Chapter 8

Attending Church for the First Time

ANN INVITED ME TO attend church with her, Faith Bible Church. She said to bring the twins because they would be able to learn children's Bible stories, which expose them to Scripture at an early age. Plus, they would have an enjoyable time.

It was another new experience, but I was looking forward to it. I had always heard to stay away from these places; nothing but crazy people there. People living in a cult, a dream world, who refuse to believe in science and have lost touch with reality. They are considered the greatest danger to civilization as we know it. And I fully embraced that line of thought until I received the letter.

Ann was introducing me to everyone; at least, it seemed that way. So many happy faces. So many humble people. So many people were interested in me. One young woman, Chris, approached me, hugged me, and welcomed me. She had this look of compassion and love in her eyes that caught my attention. She told me she remembered me from a time of demonstration in front of the abortion clinic about ten years ago.

Then it struck me. This is the woman I was screaming at and spitting in her face. This woman was praying to Jesus on behalf of these unborn children and their mothers. And I was being used by someone or something to come against her and Jesus. And now, she hugs me and welcomes me to her church, Faith Bible Church. Chris said she had been expecting me because, since that day at the demonstration, she had prayed faithfully that God would find me. I was in shock! I had no words! I hugged her neck and wept.

Finally, I was able to say over and over again, "I am so sorry; please forgive me." This is a different world; I would learn as I matured in the faith that this is a world that I would soon fall in love with. A world whose people would become my real "family." A world where I would bring my petitions and supplications to the foot of the cross, and others would pray with and for me.

These same people would become my brothers and sisters in Christ. This, as I would learn, is the body of Christ. All was made possible by the obedience of Jesus, willingly allowing Himself to be brutally crucified and then gloriously resurrected and seated at the right hand of God the Father, interceding for us, the body of Christ. I hoped that I would eventually understand this passage I heard today in Ephesians 2:4-10 which tells us:

> "But because of his great love for us, God, who is rich in
> mercy, made us alive with Christ even when we were dead
> in transgressions—it is by grace you have been saved. And
> God raised us up with Christ and seated us with him in
> the heavenly realms in Christ Jesus, in order that in the
> coming ages he might show the incomparable riches of his

grace, expressed in his kindness to us in Christ Jesus. For it is by grace you have been saved, through faith—and this is not from yourselves, it is the gift of God—not by works so that no one can boast. For we are God's handiwork, created in Christ Jesus to do good works, which God prepared in advance for us to do."

I estimated that two hundred people were in attendance at church that morning.

The song leader asked us to pick up the hymnal and find hymn #39, "The Old Rugged Cross," written in 1912. The pianist started playing, and everyone began to sing.

———◦———

"On a hill far away stood an old, rugged cross
    The emblem of suffering and shame
    And I love that old cross where the dearest and best
    For a world of lost sinners was slain.
    "So I'll cherish the old rugged cross (rugged cross)
    Till my trophies at last, I lay down
    I will cling to the old, rugged cross
    And exchange it someday for a crown."

———◦———

I was overwhelmed with joy and tears streamed down my face (again). Ann took my hand to reassure me. I realized there was nowhere I wanted to be that morning other than in the Faith Bible Church with these believers in the Lord Jesus Christ. Let the outside world criticize me, mock me, and condemn me. Their opinion and words mean nothing to me, for my true home is with Jesus and His followers. We sang another hymn, "Blessed Assurance" by Fanny Crosby, 1873.

———◆———

"Blessed assurance, Jesus is mine!
   Oh, what a foretaste of glory divine!
   Heir of salvation, purchase of God
   Born of his Spirit, washed in His blood
   This is my story, this is my song
   Praising my Savior all the day long
   This is my story, this is my song
   Praising my Savior all the day long."

———◆———

We sat down and listened to the preacher. This was my first sermon, and I did not know what to expect. The message was titled "Who Is My Neighbor?" and was based on the parable of the good Samaritan found in Luke 10:25-37.

From what I understood, my neighbor is everyone, even those who rub me the wrong way, which means I must show mercy and kindness to everyone. Well, that is impossible. Everyone does not deserve mercy and compassion. But the pastor took care of that excuse with the fact that Jesus died for us while we were yet sinners. We, including myself,

deserve death, but God showed us mercy and provided us with life."
This is when the Pastor shifted gears and really caught me by surprise.
He said, "In a room of a few hundred people, there are always some who
are not saved, who do not know Jesus as their Savior. And I want to give
you the opportunity to hear the Gospel and respond to it." *It was very
similar to the trifold that my ancestor grandfather sent to me. When the
Pastor was finished with what he called the sinner's prayer, he asked those
who said that prayer with him to raise their hands. I did not know what
to do. I wanted to raise my hand, but I just was not ready. I had too many
unanswered questions. However, after attending this church service, I did
have a greater desire to have them answered.*

The time went by quickly, and the service was closed with another
hymn, "Victory in Jesus."

———◦———

"I heard an old, old story
  How a Savior came from glory
  How He gave His life on Calvary
  To save a wretch like me
  I heard about His groaning
  Of His precious blood's atoning
  Then I repented of my sins
  And won the victory,
  Oh, victory in Jesus, my Savior forever
  He sought me and bought me with
  His redeeming bloodHe loved me 'ere
  I knew Him and all my love is due Him

38

He plunged me to victory beneath the cleansing flood."

———

What a way to end a perfect morning worshiping the Lord!

I did not want to leave. My heart was so full. Once again, I was crying with joy. All of this is a gift, a blessing, undeserved, presented to me—God's grace.

The twins ran full speed to me from their children's church class. In their sticky little hands were sheets of construction paper with drawings of what they had learned today. In their excitement, I could hear bits and pieces of how God sent an angel to save Daniel in the lion's den. What? Daniel in a lion's den? What are they talking about? My six-year-olds already knew more about the Bible than I did. Incredible.

Chapter 9

Why Did Jesus Die on the Cross?

"Ann, why did Jesus die on the cross?"

"I will start to answer that and read from my Bible this passage of scripture in John 3:16-18, 'For God so loved the world that he gave his one and only Son, that whoever believes in him shall not perish but have eternal life. For God did not send his Son into the world to condemn the world, but to save the world through him. Whoever believes in him is not condemned, but whoever does not believe stands condemned already because they have not believed in the name of God's one and only Son.'"

Ann continued, "After the fall of man in the garden of Eden, God wanted to restore man, whom He created in His image, to a personal relationship with Himself. This could not happen until the sin of man was dealt with. For God could not be in the presence of sin. God considers man His glorious inheritance as He says in Ephesians 1:18 'I pray that the eyes of your heart may be enlightened so that you may know . . . the riches of his glorious inheritance in his holy people.' And this restoration happened at the crucifixion when Jesus died and was resurrected on the third day. 'O, death, where is thy sting'? 1 Corinthians 15:55 KJV.

"Satan was defeated, sin was defeated, and death was defeated. All by the crucifixion and resurrection of Jesus. Jesus became sin for us because of His love for us. Therefore, we can now stand in the presence of God the Father because we are covered with the imputed righteousness of Jesus. When God looks upon us, He does not see our sin but sees the righteousness of His Son, Jesus Christ. God is now satisfied with this payment for man's sin, the death of his Son, Jesus Christ."

"Where does Satan come into all of this?" I asked.

"Satan or Lucifer (Morning Star) was created by God. He became very jealous of God the Father and wanted to become like God himself. Because of this overwhelming pride, Lucifer was cast out of heaven along with a multitude of angelic beings destined to occupy the earth and the underworld. Thus, we have Satan with his millions of demons.

"Satan now wages war on all human beings because he realizes the love God the Father has for them. His goal is to deceive, murder, and destroy as many people as possible so they do not become sons and daughters of God but instead spend eternity in hell, separated from God.

"Jesus described Satan in this way, 'You belong to your father, the devil, and you want to carry out your father's desires. He was a murderer from the beginning, not holding to the truth, for there is no truth in him. When he lies, he speaks his native language, for he is a liar and the father of lies.' (John 8:44 NIV). Satan knows the Scripture inside and out. He and his demons use this knowledge to accomplish their evil deeds 24/7 around the globe. Let me read from the Bible the passage that describes the end for Satan and the unbelievers, at the great white throne judgment, Rev. 20:10-15 NIV, "And the devil, who deceived them, was thrown into the lake of burning sulfur, where the beast and the false prophet had been thrown. They will be tormented day and night forever and ever. Then I saw a great white throne and him who was seated on it. The earth and the heavens fled from his presence, and there was no place for them. And I saw the dead, great and small, standing before the throne, and books were opened. Another book, the Book of Life, was opened. The dead were judged according to what they had done as recorded in the books. The sea gave up the dead that were in it, and death and Hades gave up the dead that were in them, and each person was judged according to what they had done. Then death and Hades were thrown into the lake of fire. The lake of fire is the second death. Anyone whose name was not found written in the Book of Life was thrown into the lake of fire."

Satan and all of his demons are cast into the lake of fire for eternity, along with all humanity whose names are not found in the Book of Life. This includes all the people from the beginning of time who rejected God and those after the death and resurrection of Jesus, who rejected the gospel."

I was speechless. Overwhelmed. Helpless. But hopeful.

This is why my ancestor grandparents, Marshall and Grace, sent me the "Letter of Witness" on my thirtieth birthday. It is one of God's methods of reaching out to the unsaved so they can hear the gospel of Jesus Christ and respond to it. And Satan, with his demons, will do everything in their power to keep this from happening, even after the letter has been delivered. I was starting to learn about the power of Scripture and obedience through the guidance of that small, quiet voice.

Chapter 10

Showing Ann My Birthday Gift

I FELT LIKE I was hiding something from Ann, so I decided to show her the "Letter of Witness." We were together in Ann's home for my time to ask her questions about Jesus, and I decided now was the time to show her.

"Ann, I received this envelope on my thirtieth birthday several months ago, before we met. Looking back, I realize this gift started my spiritual journey."

I handed her the short letter first. I said, "I have read this many times to myself. Would you please read it out loud so I can hear the words spoken to me?"

"Yes, of course.

January 4, 2023. Wait! Stop! Wait a minute! This letter was written to you over a hundred years ago?! And you received it this year? What is this all about, Julie?"

"My thoughts exactly, Ann. Sounds crazy. But keep reading."

"Dear Grandchild,

(I closed my eyes, and hearing these words directed to me transported me back in time. As if I am sitting in the home of my distant grandparents. Words cannot describe my feelings, wonderful, beyond wonderful.)

"We are your ancestor grandparents, Doctors Marshall and Grace Angotti. We were dentists, practicing together for forty years in Hanover, Pennsylvania, starting in 1977. We want to give you two gifts today: an uncirculated, collectors American Eagle Silver Dollar minted with 100 percent pure silver and, more importantly, the gift of eternal life, the gospel of Jesus Christ.

"As our descendant, we love you very much and want to make sure you understand this 'gift' of salvation, which is available to you. Enclosed you will find an essay in the form of a trifold, which I have written, inspired by the Holy Ghost. Grace and I have prayed for you and this moment in your life. Please read it carefully, meditate on the words from Scripture, and allow the Holy Spirit to guide you to all truth.

We leave you in the hands of the Lord.

Love with Prayers,

Marshall and Grace"

"This is incredible," said Ann. "I have never read or heard of anything like this, Julie. I don't know if I should cry, laugh with joy, or pray. Maybe all of the above."

"We are just getting started here, Ann. You'll see. Look at this coin." As I handed the silver dollar to Ann, her eyes widened with excitement.

"Would you look at this? A piece of history, and I'm holding it," Ann said. "Boy, it is heavier than it looks. This must be valuable. It's so beautiful and shiny. 'Minted in 2011.' This is hard to believe."

"Yes, it is. This is the final piece. And again, please read it out loud. My ancestor grandfather wrote this essay," I said as I handed her the trifold.

Ann began to read, **"'The Guy on the Middle Cross Said I Could Come.'** Come on, Julie, I don't know what to think of this."

"Just keep reading, Ann."

"The Gospel of Luke 23:35-43, tells of two criminals who would be executed next to Jesus: the first thief believes Jesus and goes to heaven and the second thief rejects Jesus and goes to hell. But how did this happen and what does it have to do with you?"

"You may have heard the question asked: 'If you die tonight, would you go to heaven or hell?' This passage describing the crucifixion answers this question. The first thief has died, the one to whom Jesus said, **'Today, you will be with me in paradise.'"**

In our imagination, a heavenly interview. An angel conversing with the **first thief**. The angel asks, "Why are you here?"

"I don't know," says the first thief.

"What do you mean, you don't know?" the angel says.

"I don't. I just don't know why I'm here."

"Did you go to church on Sundays?"

"No."

"Did you obey the Ten Commandments?"

"What are they?"

"Were you baptized?"

"No."

"Then why do you deserve to be in heaven?"

"The guy on the middle cross said I could come."

Ann could not contain herself anymore and started weeping. With great emotion, she said, "This is piercing my heart. I've never heard it put this way. But it is true. It's true. So simple and true."

Finally, with her emotions in check, Ann continued to read until she reached the final few paragraphs. "And how do you respond to this gift of salvation? With a simple prayer. Please, Julie, right now, say this short prayer from your heart:

> 'Lord God, (I found myself repeating these words out loud along with Ann. The Lord was speaking directly to me, and I was responding from my heart.) I confess to You that I am a sinner, and I cannot save myself. I believe You came to this earth and died on the cross for my sins. I believe You rose from the dead and are now seated at the right hand of God the Father. Jesus, please come into my heart and save me. Amen."

"If you said this prayer from your heart and you truly meant it because the Lord knows your heart, welcome to the kingdom of God."

Julie interrupted: "I did mean it, every word I said. I meant it."

Ann jumped out of her chair excitedly and joyfully, and said, "Julie, oh Julie, Jesus saved you today. He rescued you from the lake of fire. Praise God, Julie. You are saved!"

After several minutes of hugging, crying, and laughing with joy, we settled down.

"Ann, there is more to read. Please finish."

"Your position in heaven as a child of the Most High, is secure and sealed with your name being written in the Book of Life. John 10:28-29 tells us, **'I give eternal life to them, and they will never perish; and no one will snatch them out of my hand. My Father, who has given them to Me, is greater than all; and no one is able to snatch them out of the Father's hand.'**

"The Holy Spirit now indwells you and **'He will guide you to all truth"** (John 16:13). May the Lord, who created all things, bless you.

Ann stood up and began pacing back and forth with great excitement in front of Julie, talking out loud to herself. "This 'Letter of Witness' was written to Julie over one hundred years ago by her ancestor grandparents to present the gospel to her so she would have a chance for Jesus to save her. And it worked. Magnificently. God said, **'My word will not return to me empty, but will accomplish what I desire and achieve the purpose for which I sent it.'** I witnessed this verse in action right now before my very eyes. This unique method of evangelism was sent to us by the Lord Himself to reach people for Christ. Over a hundred years ago. It also proves that wherever there is Scripture, you will find the Holy Spirit convicting people of their sins and giving them the faith to believe.

"Ann, you can't stop talking about this 'Letter of Witness' slow down a little," Julie said.

"I know the Holy Spirit is putting these words in my mouth. I cannot stop talking. He won't let me," Ann said. "The first time I came up to you at the soccer game, I introduced myself and invited you to my church. I have never, ever done that to a complete stranger before. I still can't believe I did that until today. Do you remember that day?"

"Yes, I do, and I was a little shocked; no, I was a lot shocked at your forwardness. And I responded that I would think about accepting your invitation. That was not me talking. I was a mocker of everything about God. I was the last person who would want to know about God. It was that small, quiet voice inside me, influencing me."

"Exactly. That same small, quiet voice told me to go to you and say those things. It was the Holy Spirit prompting you and me. My heart is about to burst. I can't believe all of this is happening. I mean, I can, or should I say I do believe this is happening. I don't know what to say except praise God!

"Julie, do you know other family members who received this same envelope and contents?"

"I do know of one, my mother. I contacted her recently about it; she received it as I did on her thirtieth birthday. She, like me, did not know what to think of it. At the time, her married life was in complete turmoil. My father told her to sell the coin and throw everything else away. The envelope and letter made him furious. He, I recently learned, walked out on her for another woman when I was four years old. But she kept everything in that envelope safe and sound. She said something inside of her told her to do so. Over the years, she would take out the personal letter and the trifold and read them. She could not understand them, but she sensed all of it was important and it gave her a sliver of hope, however small it was.

"Then I told Ann what my mom said at the end of our conversation, 'Tell me, Julie, do you think I have another chance to know this Jesus? Is there still time for me?'"

Ann said, "This is all too much for me to comprehend. Don't tell me any more, please, Julie. We serve a great God. Scripture says, **'For my thoughts are not your thoughts, neither are your ways my ways,' declares the LORD** (Isaiah 55:8).

"I know believers who live in the same town as your mom. I will give you the information, and you can pass it on to her. Maybe you go to church with her for the first time. Tell you what, I'll go too. Make it more comfortable for everyone. Let's see what God does."

That Sunday arrived, but the twins had a bad cold and a high temperature, so I could not join Mom and Ann at church. But Mom was determined to go and meet this Jesus. She was not going to wait another day.

And that is precisely what happened. God found my mom the very first time she went to church. The Holy Spirit had been convicting her of sin and giving her the faith to believe over the last twenty-five years, a little bit more every time she took out the trifold and read all of the Scripture.

This was when I started to faithfully pray for the Lord to find my husband, James, to somehow sow the seeds of salvation by planting a few words of Scripture in his heart and mind, to bring another believer across his path to influence him for Christ just like God did for me, and to slowly give James the faith to believe.

Chapter 11

Why Pray for Others?

THE FOLLOWING SUNDAY'S SERVICE was somewhat different, but should I say, familiar. The title of the pastor's message was" Why Pray for Others?" Ann leaned over and whispered that she had spent time reading about the prayer ministry SaintsPray. This is another ministry established by my ancestor grandfather, Marshall. I had briefly discussed SaintsPray.Org with Ann at a previous time. She had passed the information on to the pastor, who was going to preach on it today. I nodded, not knowing what to expect.

The pastor started with the scripture verses he plans to focus on. He read Ephesians 6:18, NKJV, **"praying always with all prayer and supplication in the Spirit, being watchful to this end with all perseverance and supplication for all the saints."**

When he was coming to the end of the service, the Pastor said we would exchange names within the congregation to pray for each other every day, by name, for spiritual revival. The ladies would receive a pink card and the men a blue card. We don't want a man praying for another man's wife every day—too much temptation.

He said, "Print your name on the back of the card. Raise your hand if you need a pen or pencil. After that, pass the cards toward the center of the aisle, and an usher will collect them. Upon leaving the church, you will be randomly handed a card. Your instructions are to pray for the person whose card you have every day by their name for spiritual needs only. Not needs of the flesh, like employment issues, marital challenges, or health problems. Instead, pray for spiritual needs, such as those listed on the front of your pink or blue prayer card. Ask that God would, on behalf of the person you are praying for, create a desire in their heart to know Him better (Jeremiah 9:23-24); generate a heart submitted to Him (Hebrews 12:9); show specifically how to serve Him (Ephesians 2:10); and grant the courage to serve Him (Ephesians 6:19-20). I also found a great way to pray for others by reading a verse and inserting the name on your card where there is a pronoun or where appropriate. For example, Romans 6:11-12, NIV:

"In the same way, count yourselves (George Jones) dead to sin but alive to God in Christ Jesus. Therefore do not let sin reign in your mortal body, (George Jones), so that you obey its evil desires."

"This is a highly effective method of praying. Scripture is powerful to begin with. When you read it, plus insert the person's name on your card, this verse becomes a personal prayer on their behalf. Praying every day for each other by name can lead to their spiritual revival, which unleashes the power of the Holy Spirit in that person's life. He, the Spirit, knows and desires to eliminate the specific spiritual deficiencies in that person's life. All for the glory of our Lord, Jesus Christ.

"I want to tell you a few testimonies about the results of praying in this fashion. Michael was praying for his friend Roger as per instructions on this prayer card. He did mention to Suzie, Roger's wife, what he was doing, with the comment to watch for spiritual changes in her husband.

After three or four months, Michael asked Roger if the Lord was doing anything in his life and if there were any spiritual changes for him.

Roger answered, "I don't think so. No. Don't ask me questions like that."

Michael asked Roger the same questions six months later, but his wife was in the room this time. Before Roger could speak, Suzie quickly said, "I can answer that question. Every day before you started praying for my husband to grow spiritually, Roger would come home from work, shower, eat dinner, turn on the TV, and watch it until it was time to go to bed. Get up the next morning and do the same thing.

"But a few months ago, everything changed. Now Roger turns on the TV for a few minutes, gets up, and turns the TV off. He then opened his Bible and invited me to do a Bible study with him. Now, he stays up until midnight studying his Bible. My husband has become the spiritual leader of our home. I am so excited and grateful. Thank you for praying that the Holy Spirit would transform Roger."

Michael asked Roger if he was aware of his spiritual growth and maturity. And his answer was no, he was not. But in these situations, the spouse usually knows everything.

Another testimony is described by a pastor who conducted the name exchange: "Something happened that only the Holy Spirit could have masterminded. One of my deacons, Paul, came to me, showed me his blue prayer card, and said, 'Look at whose name I have, Fred Barnes. I hate this guy. I will not pray for him!' A deep-seated problem between these two men has never been resolved. Nevertheless, I explained to Paul that it was no accident that God gave him Fred's name to pray for. Give the Lord a chance, and let's see what happens. Paul reluctantly agreed. Fast forward six months. Of course, God resolved their problems, but He did much more. You see, Fred usually had to work on Sundays and came to church maybe twice a year. And wouldn't you know it, one of those times was the Sunday we did the name exchange. It gets better. I recently received a phone call from Fred, who explained that he wasn't completely honest about why he missed Sunday church. The truth of the matter is Fred wasn't required to work on Sundays but had the option to choose to work, which, of course, he did. But according to Fred, things are different now. He decided that he and his entire family needed to attend church every Sunday to hear the Word of God. So I should expect to see him regularly."

Wow! Do you see what the Holy Spirit can do if we only ask Him? And we are taking our eyes off of ourselves and asking Him on behalf of someone else. Luke 11:13 says, **"If you then, though you are evil, know how to give good gifts to your children, how much more will your Father in heaven give the Holy Spirit to those who ask him!"**

We all left church that Sunday with pink or blue prayer cards with a person's name to pray for every day. Someone has my name; they don't even know me. Maybe it's better that way.

Chapter 12

Contacting Cousin Arthur

I DECIDED TO CALL my cousin Arthur. This is the cousin who mailed the "Letter of Witness" to me on my thirtieth birthday. Wow, it has been a whirlwind since that envelope arrived. It seems like years ago, but it has only been nine months. My life is so different now, my purpose, daily thoughts, motherhood, and role as a wife. My everything. I must tell Arthur what happened to me because of that thirtieth birthday gift.

"Hello Arthur, this is your cousin Julie. The one you recently sent the 'Letter of Witness' to on my thirtieth birthday."

"Oh, Julie, I have prayed daily for you since I mailed your gift. Praying that the Holy Spirit would use that 'Letter of Witness' to proclaim the gospel to you and touch your heart. Did He touch your heart, Julie? Did He give you the faith to believe?"

Hearing those words, I immediately started sobbing, and my words began gushing out. "Yes! Yes! Jesus found me, Arthur. And He saved me. He forgave me and saved me. At first, that envelope and the letters, the coin made no sense, but something kept leading me, guiding me, and giving me the desire to want to know more. To keep asking more questions. Somehow, complete strangers who showed me love and compassion were put in my path. Even someone ten years ago, a believer I insulted terribly, but she showed her love to me by praying faithfully for my salvation. She was interested in my eternal life. She invested time in me. And we grew together as sisters, with Jesus being the common bond. I did not know this was happening at the time. But someone, something, was in complete control of what was going on."

By this time, my sobbing had stopped, and my voice had slowed and quieted to almost a whisper.

"My dear Julie, you don't know how my heart is thrilled hearing your testimony. I never know how my cousins will respond to this unique birthday gift. It is truly a miracle how the Lord draws people to Himself and the different methods He uses. I praise God daily for this ministry, WitnessForever, that He created and called our ancestor grandparents to use to serve Him and their obedience to Him when they were alive and continue to serve Him over one hundred years after their deaths."

Julie went on to explain to Arthur further how God had saved her. He found every word fascinating and glorious. He was so grateful to the Lord to be used in this ministry and to be the one who delivered this gift of salvation as a thirtieth birthday gift to his generation of cousins. Every time Arthur heard a testimony like Julie's, it reminded him of his salvation and the love the Lord extended to him. Listening to a new believer tell their story of being saved never gets old. Such enthusiasm, gratefulness, and humility. With lots of tears. Tears of joy.

"Julie, this is terrific timing. Several of your other cousins are coming over to my home in a few weeks for our yearly get-together. The Lord saved these cousins in the same fashion as yourself after receiving their

"Letter of Witness" on their thirtieth birthdays. Please bring the twins and your husband, James, if he is willing. I live in the town next to your mom. Bring her, too. I would love to see her. It's been too long."

"Yes, that sounds terrific. Let me rearrange a few things. Text me your address and the details of the day."

I had to make sure I had all the travel arrangements correct before the twins and I visited Cousin Arthur and the extended family the next day. We would walk one block to Station 14 West. We'd board any Transport Unit (TU) numbered 1123, which takes us to the Central Station. We change Units and get on TU 0023. This will take us directly to our Cousin Arthur's hometown, Central Station, where we will change units to TU 4409. This brings us two blocks from Cousin Arthur's home.

All of this travel takes precisely twenty-three minutes. Not bad for a distance of 119 miles. This is only possible because our travel lanes are in the sky. The GPS is accurate to within 1/16 of an inch in all directions for each Unit. The computer system programs each TU to travel in specific flight lanes where they can reach speeds of 300 mph quickly and safely. Our taxes pay it in full, so no boarding fee is required.

"Okay, boys, are you ready for our great adventure today? James, are you sure you don't want to come? I know it's all my family, which means loud and overwhelming. Did I say loud?"

"No, you and the boys go. Enjoy yourselves. I'll get in the way. Give everyone my love." Waving goodbye as they walked down the street, James thought, *I will stay home, away from these people with this newfound religion. What do they call them, Jesus Freaks? That's it, Jesus Freaks. And my wife is one of them. How am I going to survive this?"*

As Julie walked up the sidewalk, she saw Arthur standing in the doorway with his arms open. He is close to Mom's age, and he hugged me, hugged the boys, and shook their hands, treating them like young men.

Arthur said, "Come inside; everyone is so excited to see you today. Always a great day to see another family member who is a believer."

We walked inside and saw so many cousins that my heart jumped. They all started talking at once. "Julie, I've been praying for your salvation since you were a teenager." "Julie, I knew your thirtieth birthday was coming, and so was the Letter of Witness." "Julie, how did the Lord save you? Tell me." "Julie, Julie, Julie."

I cried, and I cried. I thought those days of crying with my salvation were over, but the tears of joy never stopped. Thank God they don't. The Holy Spirit continues to well up inside me, and it is absolutely wonderful. I turned around, and it was 4 p.m. Three hours had gone by in the blink of an eye. I have never enjoyed my cousins as much as I did today.

Chapter 13

What Did You Do With Your Salvation?

On Sunday, the pastor's sermon was titled, "What did you do with your salvation?" It focused on the judgment seat of Christ, and he started with this specific verse, 2 Corinthians 5:10: **"For we must all appear before the judgment seat of Christ, so that each of us may receive what is due us for the things done while in the body, whether good or bad.**

"This is also known as the Bema Seat. It is for BELIEVERS only, and all believers must attend. On the other hand, all UNBELIEVERS, those who rejected Christ, will be present at their judgment, the Great White Throne Judgment. For us, the believers, this is not a question about salvation. That has already been settled at the cross. Everyone standing here is saved. Every believer in heaven is there because of the death and resurrection of our Lord Jesus Christ. Is that clear? I repeat, everyone standing here in heaven at this point is saved, period.

Now, what is the purpose of this Judgment Seat of Christ? God wants to reward us for our works on earth AFTER we were saved that glorified

Him. He will also withhold our rewards for works we did not do on earth. There is no punishment here.

It's like when students attend graduation ceremonies; some receive rewards and recognition for their admirable academic achievements. At the same time, the other students do not receive these rewards or recognition. But everyone graduates and receives their diploma. Everyone is happy because all of them have diplomas. Some receive diplomas plus extra rewards and recognition for the extra efforts put forth during their education.

Another example is being a sports team member who won a championship. All the players are champions, but some received rewards and recognition for outstanding performances, much better than their teammates. They put in extra time and effort to become better athletes, which is recognized with rewards at the end of the season. But all of the players who are members of the team are considered champions.

This judgment seat of Christ is not something that will catch believers by surprise. This is not a pop quiz. We all know about it in advance or should know about it. God is giving us advance notice.

Be prepared because He is going to ask every one of us this question: "What did you do with your salvation while on the earth?"

God wants to know how much we valued our salvation. Our salvation came at a significant cost to God. It cost Him the life of His only Son, Jesus Christ. His life was freely given in a brutal death on the cross. This was the payment for our salvation. And how did we value this free gift?

This judgment is not about our eternal destiny—no, we are already saved. It is about our service to the Lord, our commitment to Him, our walk with Him, and our obedience to Him AFTER He saved us. This will demonstrate how much we value our salvation. Our life is to be lived in gratitude for this free gift of salvation.

It appears there are different kinds of Christians. What do I mean by that? Well, there are what I call secret agent Christians. This group will pray before they eat, sometimes in public restaurants. They will faithfully donate money to the church every week. They may offer intercessory prayer for others on occasion. But they rarely read their Bibles throughout the week. They do not have a ministry where they are serving the Lord. They come to church every week, follow my sermons and say all of the correct Christian cliches. But at the end of the service, they leave everything they heard that morning on the pew. They take nothing with them. As a result, they are experiencing a spiritual drought and remain very immature Christians.

These secret agent Christians aren't committed to the Lord. No. They are still committed to themselves and all the flesh has to offer—larger bank accounts, profitable financial investments, tremendous employment success, vacations, beautiful homes, and comfortable retirement. They push the Lord away with both arms, concerned only about themselves. They go through life invisible, spiritually. They keep one foot planted firmly in the world, something a French physicist named Pascal, from the seventeenth century, described as "licking the earth." Living to focus on enjoying the pleasures of this life, self-gratification.

"I worked forty-five years, and now I am retired. I plan to enjoy every minute of it. I earned it, and I deserve it!" Sound familiar?

How will these invisible Christians answer God's question when they present themselves to Him at the judgment seat of Christ? Let me give those of you who may identify as a secret agent Christian a suggestion if

I may. You still have time to do something with your salvation. You may ask how we do that. First, repent of your sins of being self-centered and ignoring God. Second, pray and ask the Holy Spirit to give you the desire to love God, to be committed to Him, and to be obedient to His Word.

Indeed, seek His face. Start to memorize scripture verses and practice saying them throughout the day. Every morning, ask the Lord, What can I do to serve you today? Give me eyes to see and ears to hear of opportunities to represent You. Put the words in my mouth when I speak of You."

This sermon struck Julie. She started to think about how she could demonstrate to God her seriousness about the value of her salvation. She is new to this being saved, but she realizes the answer is staring at her right in the face. The "Letter of Witness." She remembered reading on the WitnessForever.Org website. She can use the trifold to proclaim the gospel to her friends, past and present. To the extended family of her husband, James. And finally, as a handout to people as the Holy Spirit directs.

Is this being too bold? Will it be effective for the Lord? How brave was it for Cousin Arthur to send it to me on my thirtieth birthday? How bold was Ann to invite me to church, which was the first step in an incredible relationship? As far as being effective, what did it do for me? Absolutely everything!

From what I am learning, the idea is to put scripture in the hands of my relatives and friends. The "Letter of Witness" contains loads of great scripture. And I know that wherever there is Scripture, you will find the Holy Spirit who begins to convict people of their sins and give them the faith to believe. I must only mail or hand out the "Letter of Witness" and pray for the recipients. Trust and obey. Trust that we are God's ambassadors on this earth to accomplish His will and obey the Lord by proclaiming the gospel using the "Letter of Witness." This is too easy. How difficult is it to mail a letter?

Okay. Let me start making a list of friends. First, I need categories: work friends, mommy friends, college friends, high school friends, and other friends.

I need to send the trifold and a note explaining why they received it, something short and sweet like:

Hello, Susan. This is Julie. I have hoped to talk to you about something, but the time or circumstances were inappropriate. With that in mind, I thought a letter would be better to explain what is on my heart. And that is to help you understand the gift of eternal life, the gospel of our Lord Jesus Christ. As your friend, please allow me to present this gift of salvation that is available to you.

Family: James's aunts and uncles and James's adult cousins. What about my biological father's family? I need to ask Mom about that one.

This example note is for the family:

Hello Connie, this is Cousin Julie,

I have recently become a Christian believer and want to give you a good understanding of the gospel of our Lord, Jesus Christ. With that in mind, I thought a letter would be best. As your cousin, please allow me to present this "Gift of Salvation" that is available to you.

My professional network: MD, dentist and hygienist, optometrist, attorney, CPA, realtor, banker . . .

I will hand them an envelope with their name (or leave it at the front desk) containing the trifold and a short note, saying, "I thought you would enjoy reading this essay."

I want to be ready when God asks me, "What did you do with your salvation?"

I don't know what the rewards are, and at this point, I'm not concerned about them. My primary interest is not to disappoint God after what He has done for me. How awful that would be. I can't imagine that. I refuse to imagine that.

Chapter 14

Arthur Passes the Baton

A FEW MONTHS LATER, Arthur, my older cousin who mailed me the envelope from my ancestor grandparents on my thirtieth birthday, texted me: "Julie, I would like to speak with you about something important. Can you come to my place? We can do this at your convenience. It might be better without the twins."

Julie: "Sure, next Tuesday, the fifteenth, at 1 p.m. Does this work for you?"

Arthur: "Perfect. See you then."

"Thanks for coming to see me, Julie. How are the boys? And James, is he doing well? And your walk with the Lord? Before we start, let me pray for the Lord's blessing.

"Father in heaven, thank You for your love and kindness. Thank You for our salvation, paid for at the cross with our Lord Jesus Christ's blood and broken body. Father, we look to You for guidance and wisdom during this time with Julie and me. For it is the name of Jesus, I pray. Amen."

"Julie, I invited you to our annual get-together a few months ago so you could see firsthand the results of the original ministry of WitnessForever. There are eight cousins with whom the Lord used the 'Letter of Witness' to save them, including yourself. You are in grandchild generation number four and the last one in this specific generation to receive the gift from our ancestor grandparents, Marshall and Grace.

"I am so grateful that the Lord allowed me to participate in a small way in the salvation of all of these cousins. I had no idea what was in store for me when, at age thirty-five, I accepted the responsibility of sending the "Letter of Witness", as instructed by my predecessor but originally instructed by our ancestor grandparents, Marshall and Grace.

"Little did I know how I would be blessed by mailing out a simple envelope containing a silver dollar, a personal note, and a 'Letter of Witness.' Blessed in ways I could not imagine. Putting scripture in the hands of unsaved people and watching how alive and powerful the Word of God is as it affected their lives—watching the Holy Spirit use this scripture to convict hearts of their sin. Watching the Holy Spirit give people the faith to believe. Watching the Holy Spirit lead and guide people to all truth. Observing the transformation of the lives of our cousins to become more like Jesus. And watching these same cousins use their salvation to proclaim the gospel to others to glorify the name of Jesus Christ.

"Julie, there is one generation remaining, the fifth, that needs to receive the 'Letter of Witness,' as you did, as I did, as the previous four generations of descendants of our ancestor grandparents did. I ask you to prayerfully consider being responsible for delivering those letters to them.

"Please, I do not want an answer now. Bring this before the Lord, bathe it in prayer, and the Holy Spirit will guide you over time. Remember, you would not be sending your first letter for nineteen years because that initial cousin of the fifth generation of grandchildren is only eleven years old. This gives you many years to mature in your faith and become a humble servant of our Lord. Our ancestor grandparents decided to use age thirty for the cousins to receive their special gifts for a few reasons. One is that these children need to be adults and not live under the same roof as their parents, which could negatively influence their reaction to the letter. Also, by age thirty, they have experienced the harshness of life and realize they do not have all the answers.

"As far as the significance of the silver dollar, this is purely optional, but Marshall and Grace, like most grandparents, gave their grandchildren birthday gifts. At some point, they started to give them a silver dollar as their gift. With this gift, they would have something of value when they became young adults and independent from their parents. Marshall and Grace wanted to continue giving this gift to their future five generations of grandchildren. It would be of sentimental value to both parties involved. Plus, it might help those descendants who needed a small financial boost at that point in their lives. Those coins could increase in value significantly.

"I want to give you a narrative written by Marshall. This fully explains in detail how the ministry of WitnessForever began. Most importantly, you will see how the Holy Spirit led Marshall every step of the way. As you will read, none of this originated with Marshall. He had no personal motive that drove him. He was obedient to the instructions of the Holy Spirit, even when it went against his judgment.

"As a result, God allowed him to be used to glorify and honor the name of Jesus Christ. Marshall always pointed to the Holy Spirit for the success of every aspect of the ministry. The only people who have read this narrative are those responsible for contacting those in each generation of the grandchildren. This writing emphasizes that everything associated with this miraculous ministry, WitnessForever, is from the Holy Spirit as directed by Jesus.

"Now let me give you the same instructions I received thirty-five years ago.

"This is a list of all the next generation, the fifth and last, of grandchildren. To date, your twin boys are the last, but there is a good chance more will be born. This list has their names, birthdates, parent names, mailing address, and contact information. Of course, this information will change as the children become adults and move out of their parents' homes into their own. You will need to update your data as time goes on.

"On their thirtieth birthdays, you will send the letter to them, just as you received it. I have all the silver dollar coins, the "Letters of Witness," the personal notes, and the envelopes. Could you keep them in a safe place? You know how valuable the coins are. There are extra coins to cash in to pay for the postage and other expenses. There will be more than sixty people in this last generation. Consider recruiting three or four other cousins who are believers and received the letter on their thirtieth birthdays, like yourself. Make sure all of you keep everything confidential. Even from your spouses if they are not saved. Those silver dollars can tempt people, whether they are saved or unsaved. And you do not want to put others in a position to sin by stealing. These silver dollars and all the documents for the letters belong to the Lord. WitnessForever is His ministry. Treat it as such.

"If you allow the Lord to bless you by using you in this fashion with this ministry, I will transfer possession of everything to you. Everything stays here until then. I will leave you with the narrative I referred to. This describes how the Holy Spirit led, guided, and inspired your ancestor grandfather, Marshall. You will be amazed, as I was. This letter is meant for your eyes only."

Arthur closed in prayer.

A few days passed before I could read the narrative from Cousin Arthur. It was late one evening; everyone was in bed. Remembering what Cousin Arthur said about this writing, I would have the opportunity to peek into the mind and soul of my ancestor grandfather, almost like I would be eavesdropping on his conversations with God. This made me a little apprehensive and anxious.

With this mindset, I began to read.

I felt my phone vibrate in my pocket. When I looked at the number, I saw that it was from my hometown in West Virginia. It must be important.

"Hello."

"Marshall, this is Cousin Louis. I have some bad news. Our good friend, Frank Lopez, was killed yesterday. He was riding his motorcycle, and some guy ran over him."

"Wait. What! Where was he?"

"San Antonio, Texas."

"I can't believe it."

"Yeah, we are all shocked. I don't have much information, but I'll keep you informed. Take it easy, Cuz."

That's it? My best friend, Frankie Lopez, is dead. I felt this numbness. A wave of emotion swept over me that lasted for several seconds. This happens to me frequently—often when singing a gospel hymn in church or reading a passage in Scripture.

I had been sitting in a doctor's office as my wife, Grace, checked in for her appointment when I received the call. I decided to wait to tell her on the drive home, which I did.

Frank had a few surviving family members, and they were not willing to fly out to Texas and identify his body, resulting in a long, tedious process for his remains to be released and his estate settled. The little he had accumulated.

A few months went by, and I was contacted and informed that Frank's memorial service would be the Friday before Thanksgiving at the Catholic church we both grew up in. Now this was odd because he had been saved for thirty-five years and had not worshiped in a Catholic church since God found him. The Holy Spirit was working.

Frank and I had an agreement that whoever died first, the other was to present the eulogy containing the gospel. So I made it known that I would be speaking at the memorial service.

As the date approached, the Holy Spirit woke me up at 2:30 a.m. with specific verses I was to use and their context for the eulogy. I did not write the eulogy, but it was the work of the Holy Spirit.

Two weeks before the memorial service, I had this dream that was not a dream. Let me explain. Dreams are always herky-jerky. Nothing fits or is logical. This was different as if I were having a normal conversation with someone.

I was standing in my bedroom, and I turned around, and there was Frank, and we had this conversation:

"Frank, tell me, what is it like in heaven?"

"It's perfect. Remember what it was like when you first got saved? That feeling of euphoria, joy, and freedom? That is what it is like in heaven, 24/7. And it never gets old."

"Why do you look like you are twenty-one years old, Frank? I mean, you are skinny; you have hair and a lot of it, and you dress like Johnny Travolta in the 1970s."

"Think about it. When we were twenty-one years old, life was fabulous. Our bodies were the epitome of health, our futures were the brightest, and we were full of optimism, hope, and energy. Since you are still in the flesh, this is the best way for me to describe the perfection of life in heaven."

"Now, your memorial service is coming in a few weeks. How am I to handle that?"

"You obey. Obedience. You understand me! Obey the Spirit of God." With that said, Frank turned around and disappeared.

Grace and I drove to my hometown for the memorial service. There was an unexpected four-inch snow squall that kept some people away. We arrived at the church a little early, and I realized that since Frank and I have the same friends, we all grew up Catholics, and most of them still are. They would only come to a memorial service if it were in a Catholic church. This is why the Holy Spirit made these arrangements.

I approached the priest to remind him that I would be speaking today, and he answered: "You will not speak in my church. You can give your talk at the dinner afterward." With this, he turned around and walked away.

What little control of the situation I thought I had disappeared. *What do I do now?* I remembered Frank's parting words, "Obedience. Obey the Holy Spirit."

We sat and listened to the memorial service. This church is a large cathedral with thirty-foot ceilings, stone walls, and a cavernous interior. The acoustics are terrible, and no one could understand what the priest said, one reason the Holy Spirit did not want me to speak here. People needed to hear everything in my eulogy with the gospel presentation. Also, the Scripture I used would have contradicted many things the priest said, and he might have asked me to stop speaking. This would not be acceptable since the purpose of the eulogy was to present the gospel to people who have never heard it before—another reason the Holy Spirit did not want me to speak here.

After the service, we went to the dinner, where I would deliver the eulogy. This would be in a private room of a public restaurant where about thirty-five people showed up. A party atmosphere quickly developed, including jokes, boisterous conversations, and likely some drinking. We had one waitress for the room, a young woman in her mid-twenties with multiple tattoos and piercings, overwhelmed but doing her best.

This was not the environment where I expected to present the gospel—the opposite of a church sanctuary.

I had to focus on being obedient and ignore all the distractions to present the gospel to all these unsaved people.

I knew almost everyone in the room; I had grown up with them through my high school and college years but had not seen many of them for nearly forty years. It was an odd situation for me but a perfect one for the Holy Spirit, because He orchestrated this entire event down to the last detail, as I soon learned.

Halfway through the dinner, I stood beside my table, got everyone's attention, and started to deliver the eulogy, now the "Letter of Witness." I was coming to the end and getting ready to read the scripture of Romans 10:9-10 when the waitress walked into the room and said, "Oh, I am sorry for interrupting."

One of the men attending, who I noticed had been mocking me as I was speaking, replied to the young waitress, "Don't be sorry; you are not interrupting anything."

She immediately answered, "But I am. And I want to hear everything this man is saying," as she pointed directly at me. You could hear a pin drop. She must have been standing outside the private dining room listening intently to the gospel.

Many people asked questions after I was finished. The Holy Spirit was convicting hearts. Before leaving, I was able to ask the waitress what grabbed her attention during the eulogy. She said, "Those verses you were reading are so powerful. Where do I go in the Bible to reread everything before bed tonight?"

Another reason the Holy Spirit did not want me to speak at the church but at this restaurant.

A few people who had attended the dinner were believers and spoke with us after the eulogy. They said their ministry is to stay in the Catholic church and continue to witness to their friends and relatives. They have been praying for years for their salvation. And tonight, many of them were in this same room. They were so grateful that God would bring someone to preach a crystal clear presentation of the gospel and give everyone an opportunity to respond to it. They thanked me for my courage and obedience to the Lord to do just that. ("Obedience. Just obey!" Frank had told me.)

Wow! Driving back to our hotel, Grace and I were praising the Lord for what had just happened. I thought we had finished Frank's memorial service and eulogy, but I was mistaken.

My wife and I have a few grandchildren to whom we are forbidden to speak the name of Jesus. We have been praying for them for several years. Three weeks after the memorial service, the Holy Spirit woke me one night and spoke to my heart, "You now have a way to speak to your grandchildren about Me. Change the eulogy into a 'Letter of Witness.' Give it to them after you have died."

What? Am I in the Twilight Zone? After much prayer, the Spirit led me to fill in the blanks. WitnessForever.Org became a reality.

My instructions to make this ministry happen: I must make arrangements with a younger family member, who is saved, to mail the "Letter of Witness" with a note of introduction to all of our first generation of grandchildren on their thirtieth birthday. When they have accomplished this, they must repeat the process and pass the baton: make arrangements with a younger family member who is saved to mail the "Letter of Witness" with a note of introduction to all of the next generation of grandchildren on their thirtieth birthday. Repeat this process for as many generations as I wish. Imagine witnessing to your fifth generation of grandchildren 150 years in the future. If the Lord tarries, who knows what the spiritual condition will be then?

Arthur is correct; this narrative is impressive and inspiring. The Spirit of God is stirring my heart to accept the baton and fulfill the responsibilities of delivering the "Letter of Witness" to the Angotti's fifth and final grandchild generation. The words obedience and just obey kept ringing in my head. How could I not do this for the Lord? It is a privilege to glorify and honor His name in this fashion.

Chapter 15

James' Revelation

James thought that Julie had changed since she discovered religion. *And I must admit, for the better.* She has become a different person. She no longer nags me about picking up my clothes or continually reminds me of my procrastination to fix the leaky faucet or call my brother. She stopped telling me about my being overweight and not having that last piece of pizza. Well, she still makes comments about my lack of exercise. Julie is not perfect.

But this is quite refreshing, and I started feeling a little guilty about my behavior. I hate to admit it, but Julie was right about most of these things. I didn't want to hear about it on a daily basis. I started correcting many of my shortcomings on my own.

I opened the nightstand drawer and noticed the document Julie received on her thirtieth birthday. That envelope caused so much change in this household. I never did read it. Now is a good time. No one is around. **"The Guy on the Middle Cross Said I Could Come."**

After reading it, I did not know what to think. There are many words and concepts I am not familiar with. But one sentence caught my eye: **"The Word of God is alive and powerful, sharper than a two-edged**

sword." What does that mean? All of this stuff is over my head. It's abstract but fascinating. I am going to hang onto this document. I don't know why, but there is something here.

A few weeks later, I was finishing a two-month assignment for a mid-semester 150-page term paper. I was under a lot of pressure, and I am sure it affected my relationships with my wife and my children—and not in a good way. But all that is behind me now, and today is a special day.

"Julie, I received my grade for my mid-term paper. Do you remember the one I was struggling with and needed it to be 150 pages? Well, your terrific husband made an A-. You kept encouraging me, and I turned it all into self-pity, a short temper, and a bad attitude. You have more faith in me than I have in myself. I want you to know I recognize how you helped me, and I promise never to behave that way again.

"Julie, my sweetheart, you are awesome. To celebrate, let's have a cocktail. Shall I make your favorite vodka martini?"

"Well, you know, James, you can have a drink, but I think I will pass. I don't know what happened, but I have lost all desire to drink alcohol." *(Ann's prayer flashed through her mind, when she rebuked and cast out the demons of adultery and alcohol that were tormenting me. I completely forgot about that day. That prayer worked! I was heading full speed to complete disaster with both of those issues. But God answered Ann's prayers on my behalf. God did not want those demons plaguing me anymore, and He used Ann to accomplish that. We are God's agents on this earth to accomplish His will. And now, He chose me to be one of His agents.)*

"Wow, Julie, no more martinis for you? No more beer with the girls? No more wine with dinner? Are you sure about swearing off alcohol?

Did you think this through? Is this one of the requirements with your newfound religion?"

"No one told me I could or could not do anything, James. It's not like that. I can't explain it. I just lost my taste and desire for alcohol."

"I am sorry, Julie, I should not have brought your faith into this. I am just shocked at your decision with alcohol. I mean, come on, alcohol was the center of our lives, more in our college days, but somewhat in our married life. It's going to take some getting used to for me.

"Not to change the subject, but Julie, I must tell you I read the trifold you received on your birthday. I did not understand much of that writing, and I wouldn't mention it to you, but strange things have been happening."

Keep going, James.

"For example, last night at my PhD class, I had a brief conversation with one of my classmates, Jack, whom I never paid much attention to. You know how difficult the course load is, and there is no way we can finish everything that is expected of us. We discussed with exasperation the line we keep hearing from our professors: 'If receiving a PhD was easy, everyone would be doing it. Look around; there are not many of you.'

"Before Jack walked away, he gave me this folded card. On the front it said, 'Did You Know?' I opened it and read Hebrews 4:12,

"The Word of God is alive and powerful, sharper than a two-edged sword, piercing division between soul and spirit, bone and marrow. Judging the thoughts and intentions of the heart." John 1:14, **"The Word (of God) became flesh and made his dwelling among us. We have seen his glory, the glory of the one and only Son (Jesus) who came from the Father, full of grace and truth."**

John 14:6, **"Jesus answered, 'I am the way and the truth and the life. No one comes to the Father except through me.'** Do you know this Jesus?"

"Julie, do you have any idea what these words mean"? James asked.

"Well, James, what you read to me are three verses from the Bible. The question is, What do you think of that card?"

"I have no idea what to think of this card. It is all very confusing. I think it is nonsense. If this stuff is so important, I would already know about it. Understand it. So my answer is, 'Who cares! Except for those words, **"The Word of God is alive and powerful, sharper than a two-edged sword."** Those words intrigue me. I keep finding myself repeating them over and over in my subconscious mind. I don't know, but something inside me won't let me forget them. Whatever it is, I'll figure it out. There has to be a logical answer here. Right? And why would Jack, who I barely know, give this card to me? Strange, don't you think?"

"Absolutely. Very strange, indeed," I answered, walking away, tears of joy streaming down my face. Whispering to myself, "James, you have no idea what is ahead of you. Hang on; you are about to experience the ride of your life. Thank You, Jesus. You are awesome!"

Resources

Below are links for you to use.

Downloads are available for you.

FREE – No charge. No login information is required.

Make unlimited copies for yourself.

- The Trifold – "Letter of Witness"

  - https://www.witnessforever.org/letter-of-witness

    - WitnessForever.Org

    - Email: WitnessForever7@Gmail.com

- Prayer cards

  - https://saintspray.org/how-it-works/

    - SaintsPray.Org

    - Email: SaintsPray7@Gmail.com

Made in the USA
Middletown, DE
12 August 2024

58582819R00049